Is for Dragon Dance

by **YING CHANG COMPESTINE**

illustrated by

YONGSHENG XUAN

Holiday House / New York

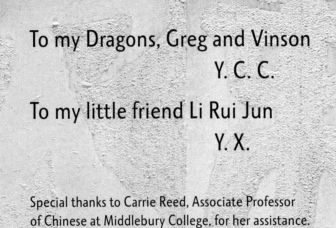

To my Dragons, Greg and Vinson
Y. C. C.

To my little friend Li Rui Jun
Y. X.

Special thanks to Carrie Reed, Associate Professor
of Chinese at Middlebury College, for her assistance.

Printed in the United States of America
The text typeface is ITC Octone Regular.
The art for this book was rendered in watercolor, acrylic, and latex.
www.holidayhouse.com
3 5 7 9 10 8 6 4 2

Library of Congress Cataloging-in-Publication Data
Compestine, Ying Chang.
D is for dragon dance / by Ying Chang Compestine ; illustrated by YongSheng Xuan.
p. cm.
ISBN 0-8234-1887-1
1. Chinese New Year—Juvenile literature. I. Xuan, YongSheng, ill. II. Title.
GT4905.C65 2005
394.261—dc22
2004058139

ISBN-13: 978-0-8234-1887-9 (hardcover)   ISBN-10: 0-8234-1887-1 (hardcover)
ISBN-13: 978-0-8234-2058-2 (paperback)   ISBN-10: 0-8234-2058-2 (paperback)

A is for Acrobats

B is for Balls

Acrobats are flexible and strong. They are masters of balance.
People watch them to celebrate the coming of the New Year.

C is for Calligraphy

Let's write the characters for "good luck."
(Don't get the ink on your new clothes!)

D is for Dragon Dance

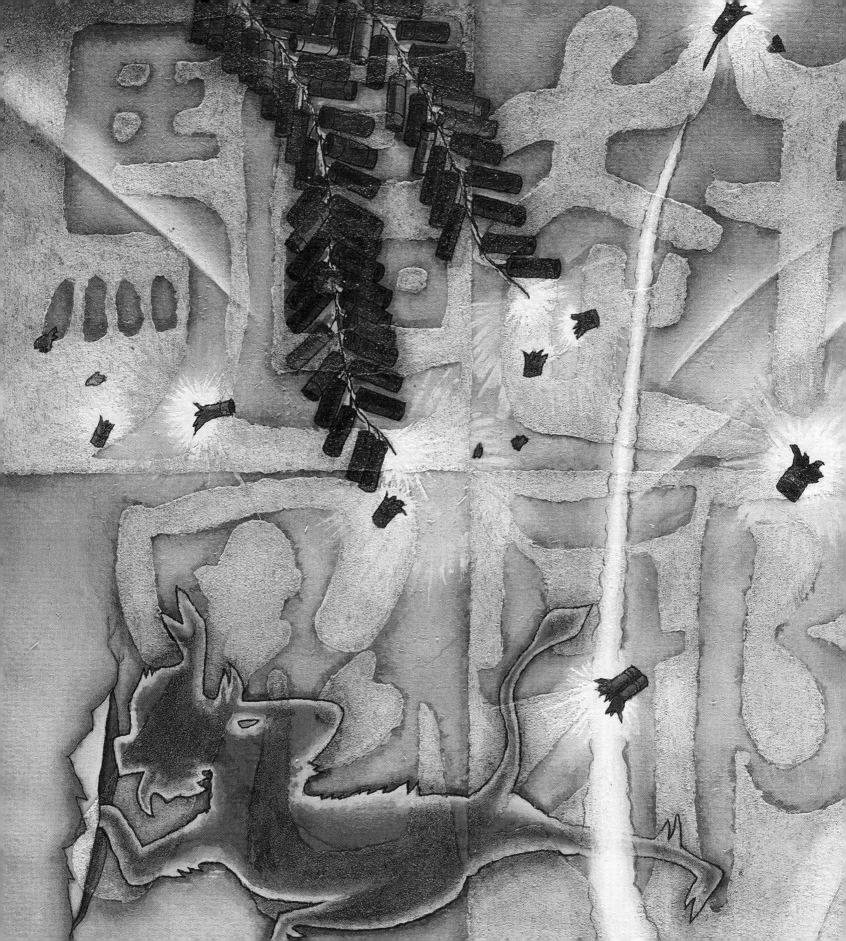

E is for Evil Spirits

F is for Firecrackers

Dragon dancers and firecrackers scare away evil spirits.

G is for Grandma and Grandpa

Grandma and Grandpa decorate their home with traditional cut paper and calligraphy to honor the New Year.

H is for Haircut

Children get their hair washed and cut, and put on new clothes for a fresh start in the New Year.

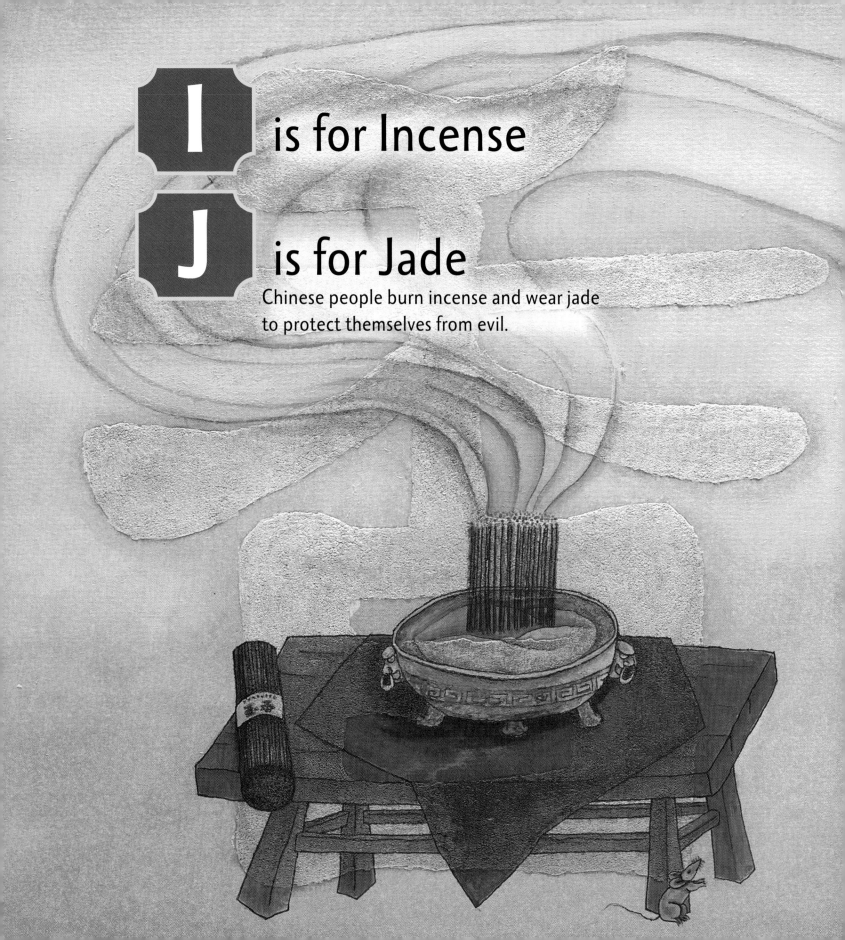

I is for Incense

J is for Jade

Chinese people burn incense and wear jade
to protect themselves from evil.

K is for Kites

L is for Lanterns

Chinese people believe that flying kites and lantern light scare away evil spirits.

M is for Moon

Chinese New Year starts with a new moon.

N is for Noodles

Eat noodles for a long, happy life.

O is for Oranges

Bring oranges to your friends' houses. They represent good fortune.

P is for Peking Duck
A whole roasted duck means happiness.

Q is for Quiz
Solve the tricky quiz and you may win a big prize.

R is for Red Envelopes
Children receive red envelopes that contain good-luck money.

S is for Steamed Dumplings
Eat these special treats to begin the New Year.

T is for Tradition

Chinese people all over the world follow similar New Year's traditions.

U is for Unity

Chinese families unite for the New Year's feast.

V is for Veneration

Families venerate their ancestors at New Year's.

W is for Wish

The New Year is a time to give good wishes.

X is for Xylograph

Wood carvings on the doors keep out evil spirits.

Y is for Yo-Yos

New Year's is a good time to play. Chinese yo-yos fly so high, they might reach the sky.

Z is for Zodiac

The Chinese calendar follows a twelve-year cycle.
Each year is represented by a different animal.
Do you know the sign for your birth date?

AUTHOR'S NOTE

The Chinese lunar calendar is based on the phases of the moon and follows a twelve-year cycle, with each year represented by a different animal. Traditions for the New Year are carefully followed during the celebration, which lasts for fifteen days. The most important part of the festivities—the New Year parades—feature dancing dragons, symbols of goodness and strength.

Tips to Ensure Good Fortune in the New Year

Clean: Tidy up and clean the house before the New Year starts. You don't want to sweep out your good fortune on New Year's Day. Get rid of old, unused items to make room for the new.

Get a Haircut: This lets everyone know you are ready for a fresh start this New Year.

Wear New Clothes: Dress in new clothes so the evil spirits won't recognize you in the New Year.

Collect Li-Shih or Red Envelopes: Children bow to elders to show their respect. In return, they are given red envelopes that contain money for prosperity in the year ahead.

Fire Away: Firecrackers frighten away evil spirits and welcome the New Year.

Meet and Greet: Visit friends and relatives and exchange treats and fruit with one another. Oranges and tangerines are said to bring health and wealth in the New Year.

Eat Dumplings: They symbolize happiness, wealth, and family togetherness.

ARTIST'S NOTE

You may notice the Chinese characters that appear in the background of each page of this book. They use four different calligraphic styles:

龍 is "Dragon" from the Song Dynasty

龍 is "Dragon" from the Wei Dynasty

龙 is "Dragon" in the Grass style calligraphy ("cursive" characters)

龍 is "Dragon" from the Han Dynasty

On some pages the characters make up Chinese sayings; on others they represent a single word.

NEW YEAR'S DUMPLING DELIGHT

Ask an adult to help you cook.

Makes 40 Dumplings

Soy-Garlic Dipping Sauce

1/2 cup low sodium soy sauce
2 tablespoons rice vinegar
2 teaspoons sesame oil
2 garlic cloves, minced
2 tablespoons green onion, minced

Dumpling Filling

10 ounces ground pork or beef
1 tablespoon fresh ginger, peeled and minced
1 cup leeks, minced
3 cups Napa cabbage leaves, minced
2 tablespoons low sodium soy sauce
1 tablespoon rice vinegar
1/2 tablespoon sesame oil
salt and pepper to taste

40 square wonton wrappers
2 large, thick carrots, peeled and cut into thin disks

1. Combine the dipping sauce ingredients in a bowl. Cover and refrigerate. Let the flavors blend in the refrigerator while making the dumplings.

2. Combine all the filling ingredients in a large bowl. Mix well.

3. Working with one wrapper at a time (cover the remaining wrappers with a damp towel to keep them from drying), spoon 2 teaspoons of meat filling into the center of each wrapper. Moisten the edges of each wrapper with water. Bring the four corners of the wrapper up over the filling. Pinch the edges together tightly. Place the dumplings, seam side up, on carrot disks in a steamer.

4. Steam the dumplings for 10 minutes or until the dumpling skins are translucent. Serve with dipping sauce.